First Riding Lessons

WRITTEN BY
Sandy Ransford

PHOTOGRAPHED BY
Bob Langrish

KINGFISHER

BOSTON

The publisher would like to thank Justine Armstrong-Smith for the use of her yard and show ponies and the Talland School of Equitation, Gloucestershire, England, and Hartpury College, Gloucestershire, England, for their invaluable help in the production of this book.

KINGFISHER
a Houghton Mifflin Company imprint
222 Berkeley Street
Boston, Massachusetts 02116
www.houghtonmifflinbooks.com

First published in hardcover in 2002
First published in paperback in 2004
10 9 8 7 6 5 4 3 2 1

1TR/0204/TWP/CLSN(CLSN)/150SMA

LIBRARY OF CONGRESS
CATALOGING-IN-PUBLICATION DATA
Ransford, Sandy.
    First riding lessons/Sandy Ransford.
        p. cm.—(Kingfisher riding club)
    Summary: Presents detailed information on beginning horseback riding lessons, including various types of ponies and horses and kinds of equipment used.
        1. Horsemanship—Juvenile literature.
    2. Horses–Juvenile literature. [1. Horsemanship. 2. Horses.] I. Title. II. Series.
SF309.2.R36 2002
798.2—dc21   2002069536

Designed and edited by BOOKWORK
Editor: Annabel Blackledge
Art Director: Jill Plank
Designer: Kate Mullins
Consultant: Nikki Herbert BHSI

For Kingfisher:
Managing Editor: Miranda Smith
Coordinating Editor: Denise Heal
Consultant: Lesley Ward
Art Director: Mike Davis
Jacket Designer: Poppy Jenkins
Additional Photography: Matthew Roberts

ISBN 0-7534-5454-8 (CL)
ISBN 0-7534-5743-1 (PA)

Printed in Singapore

Contents

Before you start

Have you ever watched riders at a horse show or simply practicing in a ring and wished you were there riding with them? You could be. Anyone can learn to ride. You just need lessons.

Participating in events

You may wish to participate in events—in showing, dressage, hunter paces, or gymkhanas. If you ride well enough, you may not need to own a pony to compete. You might be able to borrow one, or even be asked to ride for someone else.

Why take riding lessons?

Y ou may be told that if you have a quiet pony to practice on, you can learn to ride on your own. Up to a point this is true. You may learn how to make the pony move forward, turn, and stop. But compare these simple efforts with the style of a top dressage rider or with the boldness of an eventer, galloping cross-country. Whether this is your dream, or whether you just want to ride for fun, taking riding lessons will be your first step on the road to success as a rider.

Trail rides with friends

Going for a trail ride in the country with your friends is one of the most enjoyable riding activities. You can explore new places, and you may spot all kinds of interesting wildlife because animals are not afraid of horses. Your ponies, too, will enjoy being ridden out in the company of others.

Riding vacations

A riding vacation may mean pony trekking in Scotland, riding out west like a cowboy, exploring the mountains of Spain, or having intensive lessons with a professional. You will have a wonderful time on a riding vacation, and you will enjoy it even more if you are a good rider.

Where to take riding lessons

I t is important to choose a good stable when you decide to take lessons. Look for those that are approved by an equestrian organization. Try to visit several stables, and check what facilities they provide. They should be orderly and have a calm atmosphere.

Friendly instructors

The instructors at a good stable will be friendly and helpful, even if they may sometimes be firm with you! You should be able to ask them questions, and if necessary, talk to them about any difficulties you may have. When they are instructing, the instructors should wear boots and riding hats. They should also wear gloves when they are leading a horse or pony.

Happy horses

A row of clean, shiny heads looking out over their stable doors, taking an interest in everything going on, is a good sign. The ponies should look well fed, and their stalls should be clean. Overall the stables should be swept and organized.

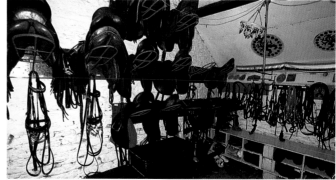

Tidy tack room

Tack has to be clean and well cared for. There should be no cracked leather, fraying girths, or stitching coming undone. Tack should be stored neatly in a tack room, ideally one which is heated in the winter, with the saddl and bridles kept on brackets and hooks.

Lessons in the outdoor arena

The stable will probably have an outdoor arena in which lessons are given. This is a fenced arena that may have a surface of rubber chips or sand, kept raked smooth and level. Even if the arena is just a fenced-off corner of a field, it should not be deep with mud.

Riding surface
The surface of an indoor arena—usually sand—stays dry whatever the weather. It must be raked smooth.

The indoor arena

An indoor arena, usually housed in a large barn, is a great asset to a stable. Whatever the weather, you can stay dry for your lessons. And during the winter it means you can ride in the late afternoons and evenings when it is too dark to ride outside.

Watching lessons
Many indoor arenas have an area where people can sit or stand to watch lessons in progress. If the indoor ring is large enough, the stable may hold competitions in it during the winter.

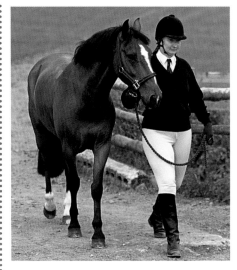

When work is over

In the summer, at the end of a long day's lessons, the ponies may be turned out into the pasture to enjoy some well-earned freedom. In the winter they are likely to be stabled at night and given feed and hay.

Clothes to wear for riding

Every sport has its competition uniform—in riding this means a shirt, a jacket, jodhpurs, boots, hat, and gloves. When not competing, riders dress more casually. The one essential item on all occasions is a helmet.

Why wear riding gear?

Jodhpurs and boots are more comfortable to wear when riding than jeans and shoes. Jodhpurs stop your legs from rubbing against the saddle; boots protect you from being knocked by the stirrups.

Body protector

For any riding activity that involves jumping you should wear a body protector. It is a rigid vest that protects your back in case you fall off.

Riding gloves with palm grips

Gloves

Riding gloves have special surfaces on their palms to help grip the reins. They may have leather or suede palms or raised rubber spots, which are useful in wet weather when reins become very slippery. You should always wear gloves when you are riding, leading, or lungeing horses and ponies.

Headgear

You must always wear a helmet when riding. You should also wear it when you are leading or lungeing a horse or pony. Whether you choose a schooling helmet or velvet-covered cap, you must make sure it is the right size. It should have a safety harness and comply with the latest safety standards.

A hunt cap has a rigid brim and is covered with fine velvet.

Casual clothes

For riding lessons or going on a trail ride you will be comfortable in jodhpurs, boots, gloves, helmet, and a shirt worn with a sweater or a jacket if the weather is cool.

Adjustable shoulder strap

A schooling helmet is a round, brimless helmet.

Safety harness

Covers are available in various colors to wear over schooling helmets.

Adjust the safety harness so that it is comfortable but holds the hat in place.

Shirt
d tie
boys
ly in
e U.S.)

Jacket

Schooling helmet with colorful cover

Fleece under jacket

Show gear
To compete in a show or any other event you should wear formal riding clothes. You may wear a black or navy blue show jacket.

Winter wear
A quilted, waterproof jacket is ideal for cold days, and half chaps help keep your legs warm. In wet weather a full-length raincoat will keep you dry.

Western gear

When showing, western riders wear a western-style shirt with a collar, jeans or western-style pants, chaps, and western-style boots with a heel. Many riders dress more casually. To protect their heads, most young riders wear helmets.

Boots

There are many kinds of boots for riding, including ankle-length, leather jodhpur boots with elasticated sides and tall riding boots, which may be made of leather or a synthetic material, and tie-up paddock boots. Long boots and half chaps protect the inner sides of your legs from being pinched by the stirrup leathers. You can wear other shoes when you are riding, as long as they are strong and have a smooth, non-ridged sole and a heel.

Jodhpur boots protect your ankles.

Riding boots reach almost up to your knees and fit tightly.

Leather half chaps may fasten with straps or zips.

Measuring a pony

Traditionally, horses and ponies are measured in hands. One hand is equal to about 4 in. (10cm), which is roughly the width of an adult's hand.

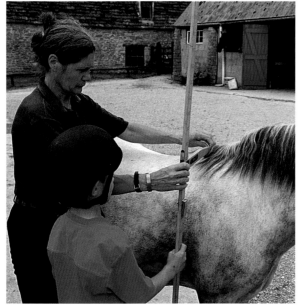

A measuring stick
An upright pole with a sliding bar enables you to read off the pony's height.

On the withers
The horizontal sliding bar rests on the highest point of the pony's withers.

Types of ponies

Ponies may be a variety of shapes and sizes. They can be so stocky and broad that your legs barely reach around them, or they may be tall and narrow. They can be hard to keep moving, or they can go like the wind. For your first lessons you need a quiet pony. As your riding improves you may step up to a more lively one.

The right-sized pony

It is important that the pony you ride is the right size for you. If the pony is too large or too small, you will be unable to use your legs properly to give the correct aids, and you may find it more difficult to balance. If you are too large for the pony, you may also be too heavy for it to carry you, and you could injure its back.

Too small a pony
This pony is too small for its rider. The rider's legs are too long to make proper contact with the pony's sides, and she may also be too heavy for the pony.

Too large a horse
This horse is much too large for its rider. The girl's legs do not reach far enough down its sides for her to be able to give the aids in the right place behind the girth.

The right size
This pony and its rider are just the right size for each other. The soles of the rider's feet are level with the line of the pony's belly, so she can give the aids properly.

A variety of ponies

During your riding career you will meet many ponies. Physically they will range from the hairy-heeled native type to the elegant, lightly-built thoroughbred type. Most will not be pure bred. Their temperaments will vary too, from sluggish to highly excitable. Some ponies will need more experienced riders than others.

Typical beginner's pony
A first pony might be a native breed or crossbred. It will be quiet and dependable.

Crossbred pony
A crossbred pony means that its parents are from different breeds. For example its mother is a welsh pony, and its father is a quarter horse. This pony would suit a competent rider and could carry out most activities.

Thoroughbred-type show pony
This kind of pony has beautiful gaits and goes well in the show ring. It would need an experienced rider.

Purebred native pony
A pony such as this Welsh Section A (Welsh Mountain) is an ideal all-rounder for a fairly experienced rider.

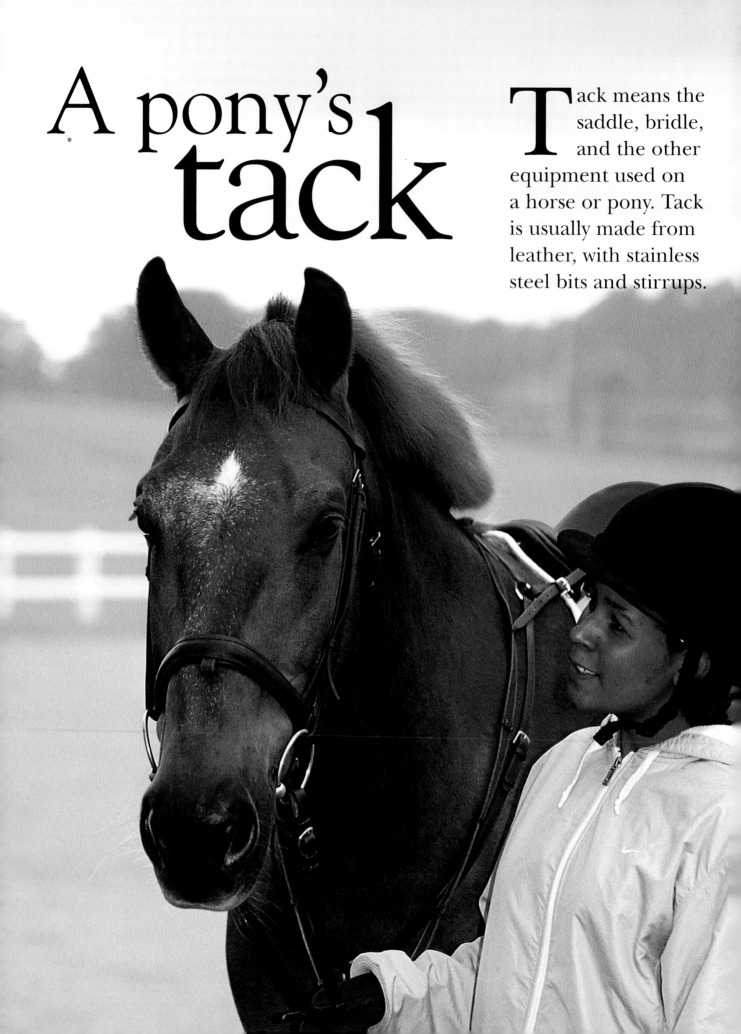

A pony's tack

Tack means the saddle, bridle, and the other equipment used on a horse or pony. Tack is usually made from leather, with stainless steel bits and stirrups.

Saddles and girths

Y ou need a saddle to give you a secure and comfortable seat on a horse's back. The girth holds the saddle in place. Saddles are made on a rigid frame called a tree. A canvas seat is stretched across the tree and the padded seat goes over that. Saddles are made in different sizes and widths to fit horses of different sizes.

Types of saddles

Saddles are made in different styles according to the use for which they are intended. Mostly you will use some kind of general purpose saddle, but if you go on to take part in equestrian sports, you may need to use a special saddle.

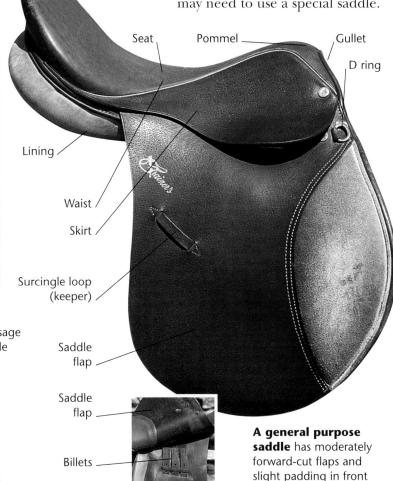

Cantle
Seat
Pommel
Gullet
D ring
Lining
Waist
Skirt
Surcingle loop (keeper)
Saddle flap

A general purpose saddle has moderately forward-cut flaps and slight padding in front of the rider's knees. It is comfortable and suitable for most riding activities.

Saddle flap
Billets
Buckle guard

A dressage saddle has straight flaps and a deep seat. It often has extended billets so that the buckles do not get in the way of the rider's leg contact with the horse.

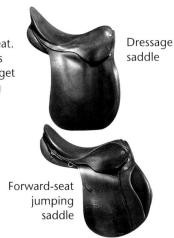

Dressage saddle

Forward-seat jumping saddle

A forward-seat jumping saddle has forward-cut flaps and padding in front of the rider's knees (knee rolls) and behind their thighs (thigh rolls) to help keep their legs in the right position when jumping.

Types of girths

Girths may be made from leather, webbing, or synthetic fibers. Webbing girths were traditionally used in pairs. Leather girths, which may be made from a folded piece of leather or shaped to avoid pinching near the horse's elbows, are expensive but last a long time. String girths are inexpensive but can pinch the horse's skin. Padded synthetic girths are comfortable and easy to maintain. For safety, girths should be fastened on either the front two or the front and back billets.

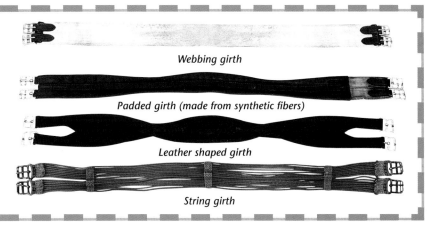

Webbing girth

Padded girth (made from synthetic fibers)

Leather shaped girth

String girth

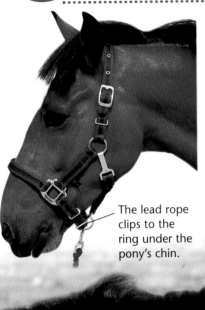

Halters

Halters are put on horses' or ponies' heads to lead them and to tie them up. They may be made of nylon or leather. People tend to use nylon halters around the stable and keep leather ones for special occasions.

The lead rope clips to the ring under the pony's chin.

Bridles and bits

A bridle and bit are the means by which a horse or pony is controlled by its rider. Bridles are traditionally made of leather in three sizes: full size, cob, and pony. Today other materials are also used. There are two main kinds of bits—snaffle and curb—though there are many different varieties. Bits are usually made of stainless steel.

Snaffle bridle

A snaffle bridle, which has a jointed snaffle bit and single reins, is the kind most often used. The headpiece buckles onto cheekpieces, which hold the bit in place. A separate headpiece is attached to the noseband and fastens on the left.

Throatlash stops the bridle from slipping forward.

Cheekpiece holds the bit in place.

Noseband

Stop, to keep the ring of a running martingale away from the bit.

Eggbutt snaffle bit

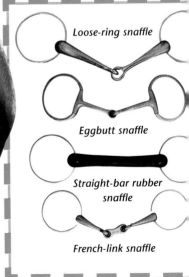

Loose-ring snaffle

Eggbutt snaffle

Straight-bar rubber snaffle

French-link snaffle

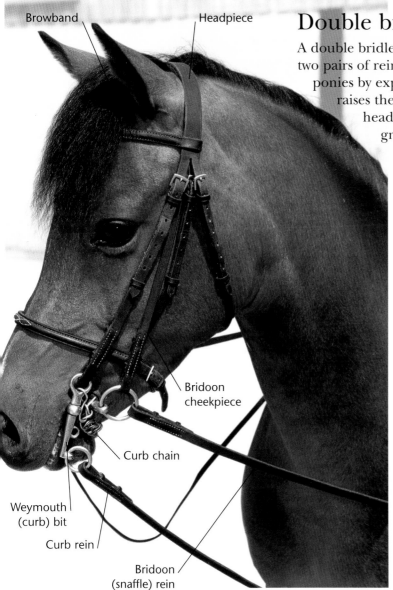

Browband

Headpiece

Bridoon cheekpiece

Curb chain

Weymouth (curb) bit

Curb rein

Bridoon (snaffle) rein

Double bridle

A double bridle has both a snaffle bit and a curb bit and two pairs of reins. It is used only on well-trained horses and ponies by experienced riders. The snaffle bit, or bridoon, raises the horse's head. The curb bit lowers the horse's head. The curb chain, tightening in the chin groove, gives extra control.

Bit converters

Short leather straps that connect the curb and bridoon rings of a pelham bit, allowing single reins to be used with it, are called bit converters. Their use means that the two functions of the bit cannot be separated, but some horses go well with them.

Running martingale
This attaches to the girth at one end. It passes through a neck strap and then divides into two straps that end in rings through which the reins pass.

Standing martingale
Like a running martingale, this also attaches to the girth and passes through a neck strap, but the single strap is then fastened to the back of the noseband of the pony's bridle.

Martingales

Martingales are used to stop a horse carrying his head too high and evading the rider's control. They also prevent it from throwing its head up in the air and possibly hitting the rider in the face. They should be fitted with care. They must not be so tight that they pull the horse's head down.

Types of bits

A snaffle bit consists of a mouthpiece—usually jointed—and two rings. A curb bit has cheekpieces that rotate to put pressure on the headpiece of the bridle. It also has a curb chain, which presses on the curb groove and is held down by a lip-strap.

The two bits of a double bridle are the bridoon (snaffle) and Weymouth (curb).

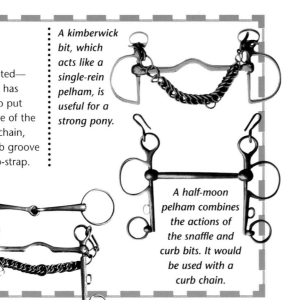

A kimberwick bit, which acts like a single-rein pelham, is useful for a strong pony.

A half-moon pelham combines the actions of the snaffle and curb bits. It would be used with a curb chain.

Tying a quick release knot

When tying up a pony, fasten its lead rope to a loop of string or a ring using a quick release knot.

Loop the lead rope, and put it through the ring. Twist the rope a few times.

Make another loop in the end of the rope, and push it through the first loop.

Tighten the knot by pulling on the halter end. Pull the free end to undo it.

Putting on a halter

You will need to put a halter on a pony in the stall so you can tie it up while you are grooming, tacking up, and mucking out. You will also need to use a halter to catch the pony and lead it back from the pasture.

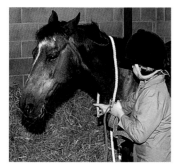

1 If the pony is outside or if it is likely to wander around the stall, first put the lead rope around its neck so you can hold on to it if you need to do so.

2 Put the noseband over its nose. Hold the cheekpiece of the halter in your left hand. Reach under its chin with your right hand to grasp the headpiece.

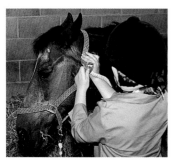

3 Bring the headpiece over the pony's head and fasten the buckle, tucking in the end of the strap. Tie up the pony using a quick release knot.

Saddling up

When you have your first riding lessons your pony will be tacked up for you— that means it will have its saddle and bridle on. But you will need to learn how to do this by yourself. Start by tying the pony up in the stable or its stall, and then get its tack. You can hang the bridle on a hook or over the door while you saddle up.

Carry the bridle over your shoulder.

Carry the saddle over your arm with the pommel resting by your elbow.

Run the stirrups up the leathers.

Carry the girth over the saddle.

Carrying tack

To avoid trailing the reins on the ground, loop them up and put them with the bridle over your shoulder. Carry the saddle on your left arm, supporting it with your right hand. It is then in position for saddling the pony.

Putting on a saddle

The saddle sits just behind the pony's withers, and the girth goes around in the shallow groove just behind its forelegs. You put the saddle on from the pony's left side, but you must go around to the right side to fasten on the saddle pad and check that the girth is correctly buckled on that side and not twisted.

1 Hold the saddle pad in both hands, and lower it onto the pony's back in front of where it will eventually go.

2 Put the saddle on top of the saddle pad, and then slide them back together until they are in the right position.

3 Take the front billet out of the buckle guard and slide it through the loop on the saddle pad's strap.

4 Put the front billet back through the buckle guard. Repeat steps three and four on the left side of the saddle.

5 Let the girth hang down on the right side, and check that it is not twisted.

6 Go back to the left side of the pony, and reach underneath its belly to grab hold of the end of the girth.

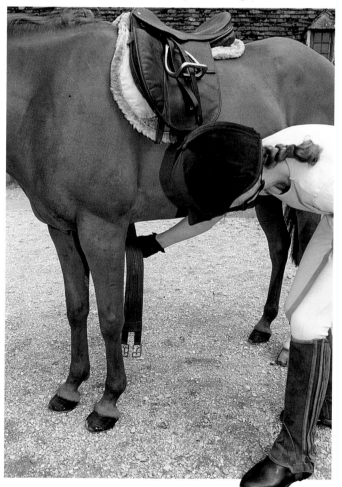

7 Fasten the girth buckles on the front two or the front and back billets. Smooth the skin under the girth.

Slide the guard back down over the girth buckles.

Putting on a bridle

A horse's or pony's head is very sensitive, so you must always handle it gently when putting on its bridle. Be careful not to brush your arm or the bridle's cheekpieces against its eyes. Do not pull on its mouth when you put in the bit. If you do it slowly and gently, putting on a bridle is not as difficult as it may appear.

How to put on a bridle

When you are learning, a bridle appears to be a very complicated piece of equipment. The key to being able to put it on without getting confused is to hold it up by the headpiece and take a good look at it. The headpiece goes over the top of the pony's head, and the cheekpieces support the bit. The browband stops the headpiece from slipping back, and the throatlash stops the bridle from slipping forward.

1 Carrying the bridle, approach the pony on its left side and undo its halter. Slip the halter off its head, and then refasten the headpiece around the pony's neck.

Checking the fit

A horse or pony usually wears the same bridle each time it is ridden, so it should fit properly without needing much adjustment. But you need to know how the bridle should fit to be sure it is correct.

Before you put the bridle on check that the noseband is level. If it is not, straighten it out by easing the headpiece through the browband, pushing it up on one side, and pulling it down on the other.

The cheekpieces should be buckled onto the bridle's headpiece at the same number hole on each side. If they are not, the bit will be pulled up more on one side than on the other.

When the noseband fits correctly, it should lie halfway between the pony's cheekbone and its mouth. There should be enough room for you to slide two fingers between the noseband and the pony's nose.

When you have fastened the throatlash, there should be room for your whole hand to pass between it and the pony's cheek. If the throatlash is too tight, it may interfere with the pony's breathing.

A snaffle bit should slightly wrinkle the corners of a pony's mouth when it is at the correct height. You can adjust the height of the bit by altering the length of the cheekpieces on each side of the bridle.

6 Pull out the pony's forelock from under the browband so it lies nicely over it. Smooth out any parts of the mane that are caught in the headpiece.

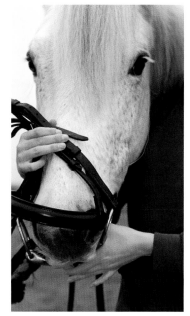

2 Hold the bridle in your left hand by the headpiece. Take hold of the reins in your right hand, and put them over the pony's neck.

3 Put your right arm under the pony's jaw, and hold the bridle in your right hand. Holding the bit flat on your outstretched left hand, press it against the pony's lips.

4 If the pony does not want to open its mouth, wiggle your left thumb in the corner where it has no teeth. Press the bit against its lips as you do so.

5 When the bit is in the pony's mouth, put the bridle's headpiece over its ears, folding the ears down to enable you to do so.

7 On both sides of the bridle, check that the browband is not so high up that it is pressing against the base of the pony's ears.

8 Reach under the pony's jaw to the right-hand side of the bridle for the throatlash. Check it is not twisted, and then bring it under to the left side of the bridle, and fasten the buckle.

9 Check that the bridle's noseband is not caught up on the cheekpieces, and then fasten it behind the pony's jaw. Push the end of the noseband strap firmly through its keeper.

10 Do a final check on the bridle. Make sure that the buckles are fastened correctly and the ends of all the straps are in their keepers.

Saddle blanket

The horse wears a thick woolen blanket or pad under the saddle to protect its back from being rubbed. Traditionally these blankets were handwoven from sheep's wool and doubled as bedrolls.

Western saddle

A traditional western saddle weighs 40–50 lbs (18–22.5kg). Most modern saddles are lighter, but they all feature the horn at the front, to which steers were roped, and the high cantle at the back. The girth is called a cinch.

Western stirrups
A stirrup is made from a single, curved piece of wood or plastic.

Western tack

Western tack was designed for a cowboy's horse. The saddle was the cowboy's home. It had to be comfortable and carry belongings—from bedding and food supplies to ropes and a rifle. The bridle had long reins. When they trailed on the ground, the horse was trained to stand still as if tied up.

Horn

Cantle

Flank strap

Skirt

Fender made of decorative leather

Seat jockey

Front rigging

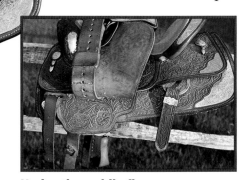

Under the saddle flap
When you lift the saddle flap, you can see the broad, leather strap that carries the stirrup. The outer fender covers the strap and protects the rider's leg.

Putting on the saddle

If you are small, you may need help to carry and put on a western saddle. It takes a lot of strength to lift it up onto a horse's back and settle it in place. Never "throw" the saddle on, like you see in some movies, because this would upset the horse.

1 First put the saddle blanket on, and then lower the saddle onto the horse's back.

2 Check that the cinch is not twisted on the right side, and then fasten it on the left side.

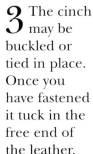

3 The cinch may be buckled or tied in place. Once you have fastened it tuck in the free end of the leather.

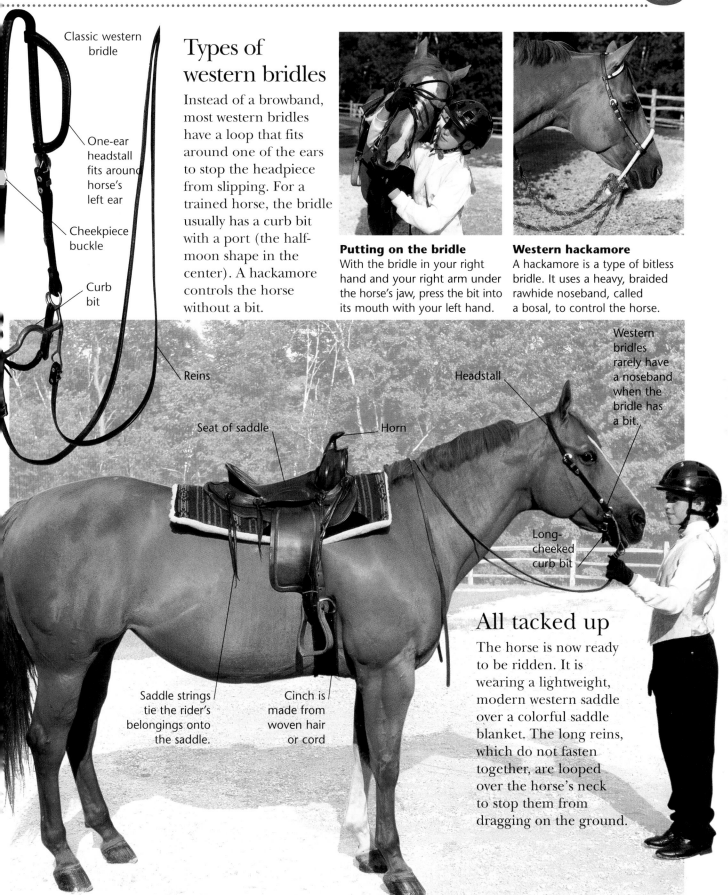

Classic western bridle

One-ear headstall fits around horse's left ear

Cheekpiece buckle

Curb bit

Types of western bridles

Instead of a browband, most western bridles have a loop that fits around one of the ears to stop the headpiece from slipping. For a trained horse, the bridle usually has a curb bit with a port (the half-moon shape in the center). A hackamore controls the horse without a bit.

Putting on the bridle
With the bridle in your right hand and your right arm under the horse's jaw, press the bit into its mouth with your left hand.

Western hackamore
A hackamore is a type of bitless bridle. It uses a heavy, braided rawhide noseband, called a bosal, to control the horse.

Reins

Seat of saddle

Horn

Headstall

Western bridles rarely have a noseband when the bridle has a bit.

Long-cheeked curb bit

Saddle strings tie the rider's belongings onto the saddle.

Cinch is made from woven hair or cord

All tacked up

The horse is now ready to be ridden. It is wearing a lightweight, modern western saddle over a colorful saddle blanket. The long reins, which do not fasten together, are looped over the horse's neck to stop them from dragging on the ground.

First lessons

The first time you sit on a pony you will probably feel a little strange. As you have more lessons you will begin to feel at home on its back. Your first pony will be a very quiet one, and it will help your instructor take care of you.

Meeting your pony

W hen you go for your first riding lesson, your instructor will introduce you to the pony you are going to ride. It is a very exciting moment—although you may feel a little nervous. If you do, try to hide it from the pony. Ponies quickly sense how someone is feeling and react to it. If you are anxious and upset, or worried, your pony will become anxious too. If you act in a positive way, your pony will have confidence in you.

Greeting a new friend

When you meet a strange pony, walk up to it confidently. Hold out the back of your hand with your fingers curled into your palm, and let it sniff at it. Speak to the pony, and give it a pat on the neck.

Getting ready
If you are having a group lesson, you will probably lead your pony to the arena and then mount there. Before you mount, you or your instructor should check the pony's tack. Your instructor will probably help you mount by holding the pony.

Setting off
If you mount before the arena, the group will set off for the arena when all the riders are on their ponies and have checked their girths and the length of their stirrups (see pages 30–31).

Your first lessons

You may have private riding lessons or lessons with a group of other beginners. Either way, your instructor or an assistant may lead your pony with a lead line. This clips on to the pony's bit rings, leaving you to hold the bridle's reins.

Getting to know a pony

Before you can handle and ride ponies you need to know a little about them. Ponies are gentle, nervous animals, happiest in a group. If something frightens them, their instinct is to run away. Living naturally in a herd, they follow a dominant pony. When we domesticate them we take that animal's place, and once they trust us they will do as we wish.

Approach with confidence

When you approach a pony, talk to it in a friendly way. Give it a pat on the neck or a treat, and handle it quietly and firmly. It will then feel confident. If you are nervous, hesitant, or pushy, it will be upset and may behave badly.

How to lead a pony correctly

You lead a pony on its left side. Hold the lead rope or reins in your right hand up by the pony's head, and take the other end in your left hand. Walk forward in a positive way beside the pony's shoulder without looking back at it.

Tips for handling horses and ponies

Speak to a horse or pony in a calm and friendly way as you approach it.
Approach toward its shoulder, from the front, where it can see you.
Never shout, rush around, or make sudden movements near horses or ponies.
Be gentle but firm when you are handling horses and ponies.
Try to follow the same routine around the stable and with the horse each day.

Natural behavior

Wild ponies live in herds. If you turn a pony out in a pasture, it will immediately gallop off to join the others. If one pony shies from an object, the others will copy it.

Nervous or naughty?

A pony that hesitates about passing an unusual object may be frightened. Give it the benefit of the doubt and let it have a good look at the object. Then drive the pony firmly forward with your seat and legs, keeping the pressure on until the pony has passed the object.

Gaining control

Once the pony walks past the object relax your aids, and reward the pony. Pat it on the neck and tell it what a good pony it is. If it refuses to pass the object, take the pony around in a circle and approach it again, reinforcing your aids with a crop if necessary.

Mounting block

Mounting blocks give you extra height and stop you from pulling the saddle over.

Hold the reins in your left hand, and put your left foot in the stirrup. Spring off your right foot with your right hand holding the saddle.

Swing your right leg over the horse's back, and lower yourself into the saddle. Put your right foot in the stirrup, and then take up the right rein.

Getting a leg up

Hold the reins in your left hand, and put your right hand on the saddle. Your helper holds your left leg.

With your helper supporting your left leg below the knee, decide when they will lift (such as on the count of three). Lift yourself with your arms while your helper propels you up.

When you reach the level of the saddle, swing your right leg over it and sit down. Straighten your back, put both your feet in the stirrups, and then take up the reins in both hands.

Mounting

Mounting means getting on a horse or pony. Although you may have help at first, you will need to do it alone. When you are out riding, you may have to dismount to open a gate, for example, and you have to be able to get back on again. If you find mounting difficult because you are not very strong and lack spring or because you are not very tall, try letting the stirrup leather down a hole or two.

How to mount

There are various ways of mounting a pony. You may be able to use a mounting block or to get a leg up, but you will also be taught the correct way to mount. When you are learning, you should have a helper hold your pony. When you are on your own, you can stop your pony from walking forward by standing it to face a wall or gate.

1 Stand on the pony's left side, facing its tail. Hold the reins in your left hand. With your right hand, turn the stirrup toward you and put your left foot in it.

2 With your left hand resting on the pony's withers, grasp the waist of the saddle with your right hand and at the same time spring up off your right foot.

Turning the stirrup

It is important that the stirrup iron and leather are turned the right way when you are riding. If they are not, the edge of the stirrup leather presses into your leg. This is very uncomfortable and prevents you from using your legs properly.

Before you mount, turn the back of the stirrup iron toward you. As you mount and twist your leg and foot around the stirrup turns so it ends up facing the right way.

To put your right foot in the stirrup, turn the front of the iron out. You may do this with your hand at first, but with practice you will be able to use your foot.

Western style

Start by facing the horse's left side. Hold the reins in your left hand, resting on the horn of the saddle. Put your left foot in the stirrup and your right hand on the back of the saddle. Spring up off your right foot. Swing your right leg over, being careful not to catch it on the high cantle. Lower yourself gently into the saddle. Put your right foot in the stirrup, and take the reins in your right hand.

3 Swing your right leg up and over the pony's back, being careful not to kick it with your toe as you do so. It is helpful if someone leans on your right stirrup as you mount to stop you from pulling the saddle over to the left when all your weight is on that side.

4 As you bring your right leg over the saddle, slide your right hand out of the way. Lower yourself down gently—do not flop.

5 Slip your right foot into the right stirrup, pointing your toe in as you do so. Take up the reins in both of your hands.

Dismounting

The method of dismounting that starts with both feet out of the stirrups involves a certain amount of gymnastics. Most people consider it the best way to get off a horse because it is the safest. The most dangerous thing that can happen to a rider is to be dragged along the ground by a moving horse because one foot is stuck in a stirrup. By taking both feet out of the stirrups and then jumping clear, you land on both feet at the same time and can walk with the horse.

How to dismount

When dismounting, you vault off the pony in one easy movement, so you have both feet on the ground very quickly and can walk beside the pony if it moves. As you land beside the pony be careful to keep your own feet out of the way of its front hooves so it does not tread on you. Before you dismount, check that you are not going to land on uneven ground and risk hurting your feet or ankles when they take your weight.

1 Bring the pony up to a good, square halt (see page 36) on a level piece of ground. If you think it may walk forward, face a gate. Still holding the reins in both hands, take both feet out of the stirrups.

1 Hold the reins in your left hand, and put your right hand on the pommel. Then take your right foot out of the stirrup.

Alternative way

An alternative method is to take your right foot out of the stirrup first and then vault off to land on both feet together. Unless the pony is trained to stand, you should get someone to hold it while you dismount this way.

2 Pass the reins and crop, if you are using one, to your left hand. Rest them on the base of the pony's neck, just in front of the withers.

2 Swing your right leg over the pony's back, and put your right hand on the waist of the saddle. Take your left foot out of the stirrup and vault off.

3 Slip to the ground, landing on both feet and bending your knees slightly as you do so. Then with your right hand take hold of the reins by the bit so you can lead the pony.

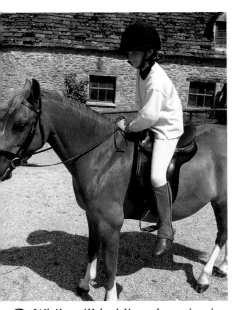

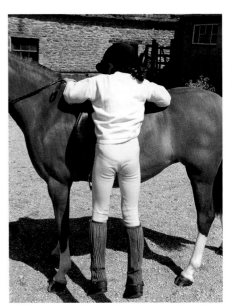

3 While still holding the reins in your left hand, put your right hand on the pommel of the saddle and lean forward.

4 Swing your right leg up and bring it over the pony's back, being careful that you do not kick the pony as you do so.

5 Slip to the ground, landing lightly on both feet and bending your knees. Take hold of the reins near the bit in your right hand.

How to sit in the saddle

W hen you sit on a horse or a pony, you should be relaxed and comfortable yet alert and ready for action. You should sit deep in the saddle with your back straight and your thighs and lower legs in contact with the saddle and the pony. Your body should be supple enough to follow all of its movements.

How to hold the reins

Hold your hands in a relaxed position in front of you with the thumbs up and the palms of your hands facing each other. Then take up the reins. Single reins should pass between your pinky and ring fingers, up through your hands, and between your thumbs and first fingers.

Diagonal line

When you are sitting on the pony your arms must be in the right position. If you are holding the reins correctly, the reins and the lower parts of your arms should form a straight, diagonal line running directly from the pony's bit back to your elbows.

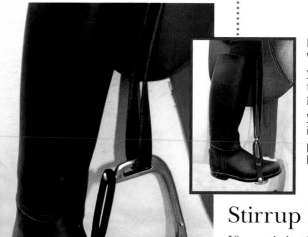

Foot position in stirrup

When you are putting your foot in the stirrup, turn the front edge of the iron out. Rest the ball of your foot on the stirrup iron, and keep your toes pointing forward and your heels pressed down.

Shortening reins

Hold both reins in your right hand while you slide your left hand down to the length you want. Then hold both reins in your left hand, and slide your right hand down to shorten the right rein to the correct length.

Stirrup length

If you sit in the saddle and let your legs hang down naturally, the stirrups will be approximately the correct length when they hit you at your ankles. You may need them a couple of holes shorter than this to start with and when jumping.

Keep your head up and look straight ahead between the pony's ears.

Keep your upper arms relaxed, and hold them close to your body.

Sit up straight, but do not hold your back stiffly.

Keep your seat in contact with the saddle, and do not lean back.

Keep your heels down and your toes up.

Vertical line

When you are sitting in the saddle, imagine a straight vertical line running down beside you. If you are sitting in the correct position, the line would start at your ear and pass down through your shoulder and hip before eventually finishing at the level of your heel.

Checking the girth

You should check the girth before you mount, but it is a good idea to check it again after a few minutes' riding. Some ponies blow themselves out when they are saddled and their girths are being tightened. Later when they have relaxed, the girth may be too loose. You can adjust it from either side.

Keeping hold of the reins, lean forward to slide your fingers under the girth. If you can get more than two fingers between the girth and the pony, then you need to tighten the girth.

Put your left leg forward, lift the saddle flap, and pull up the billets one at a time to tighten them.

Adjusting the stirrup length

You can adjust your stirrups while mounted, keeping your feet in them as you do so. With practice you can do this by touch alone, without looking down.

Holding the reins in one hand, pull up the end of the leather with the other.

Undo the buckle, slide it to the correct position, and put the prong in the hole.

Pull down the underneath part of the leather to slide the buckle up again.

The aids

The aids are the signals a rider uses to communicate their wishes to a horse or pony. The aids are divided into natural aids—the rider's legs, hands, seat, and voice—and artificial aids—crops and spurs. A well-trained horse responds to the lightest of aids, but some ponies may need stronger ones.

Hand position
Keep your fingers closed while you keep an even contact with the horse's mouth.

Boot with spur fitted

Spurs are attached to riding boots with leather straps.

Artificial aids

There are various kinds of crops. Long crops are used for dressage and schooling; short crops for ordinary riding; and leather-covered crops for showing. Both crops and spurs are used to reinforce leg aids, although spurs should be used only by experienced riders.

Dressage crop

Normal crop

Jumping bat

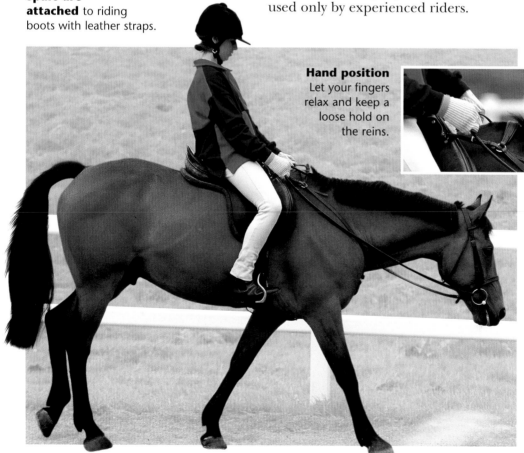

Hand position
Let your fingers relax and keep a loose hold on the reins.

Riding on a loose rein

At the end of a ride and at intervals during a lesson it is a good idea to let the horse walk on a loose rein to stretch its neck muscles and relax. When you are riding on a loose rein, you still need to keep your lower legs in contact with the horse's sides, but you can ease the pressure on the reins. However, you must always be ready to gather up the reins quickly if something startles the horse.

Medium walk

Maintain a feel on the horse's mouth through the reins. With your lower legs, squeeze its sides behind the girth to tell it to walk forward.

Leg position
Keep your heels pointing down and your lower legs pressed into the horse's sides.

Driving forward

Sometimes ponies dislike or are afraid of particular objects and refuse to pass them. When this happens, keep a firm hold of the reins and use your legs really strongly to drive the pony forward.

Using a crop

If the pony does not pay attention to your leg aid, you can reinforce it with a tap of the crop just behind the girth. A pony that misbehaves can also be given a sharp tap with the crop in the same place.

Expert rider

If you watch an expert rider performing a dressage test you will hardly notice any aids being given. The lightest of touches and slight shifts of weight in the saddle are enough to instruct the horse to carry out the most complicated movements.

A dressage rider rides with long stirrups.

This dressage movement is called a piaffe. It is like trotting in place.

"Leg into hand" is the aim of riding. The legs drive the horse forward; the hands control the energy created.

First-time rider

On the lead line the instructor has direct control of the pony. To help the rider feel safe on their first lesson, the instructor will tell them to hold on to the front of the saddle or a neck strap.

On the lunge or lead line

Your first few riding lessons are likely to be on the lunge or on a lead line. The instructor controls your pony, leaving you free to concentrate on sitting correctly and applying the aids. A lunge line is a long rein attached to a special halter that the pony wears over its bridle.

Starting out
As the horse walks around in circles the rider steadies themself by holding on to the front of the saddle.

Gaining confidence
Once the rider feels secure, they let go of the saddle and hold the reins in the correct position.

On the lunge

Riding on the lunge is a good way of learning to balance on the horse and to build up your confidence. It enables you to practice using the aids without having to worry about the horse's speed or direction.

Tips for first lessons

Get comfortable in the saddle before you start. Make sure that your stirrups feel right and that the ends of the leathers are not sticking into your legs.

If you feel insecure, hold on to the front of the saddle or to a neck strap.

Try to relax. Let your hands follow the movement of the pony's head.

Off balance

If you lose your balance when you are first learning to ride, it is tempting to try to hang on by pulling on the reins. You should never do so, however, as you can damage the pony's mouth and may make it very sore.

Trying too hard

When you first ride a horse or pony, you must try to remember many things, but do not try so hard that you hold your body stiffly. Try to sit easily, and let your body and hands follow the horse's movements.

Holding the reins
You can rest your hands on either side of the horse's withers to help you balance.

Halter
The horse may wear a halter to lead it by.

Using your legs
Squeeze with your legs behind the girth to keep the horse walking on.

Walking slowly
At first the instructor will lead the horse around at a slow walk.

On your own

W hen you first ride off the lunge or lead line, you will learn how to make your pony walk and halt. This is not as easy as it sounds. The aim is to make the pony walk purposefully and with energy and to halt when you tell it to do so. The pony should be balanced, alert, and responsive to your aids at all times.

Square halt

To achieve a square halt, sit deep in the saddle with the horse's front and hind legs in line. Lean your weight backward slightly, and gently hold back on the reins. The pony is standing still, but it should be full of contained energy, ready to set off again.

Keep a contact
Although you have stopped keep your leg against the pony's sides, and keep hold of the reins.

Hind legs
A gentle nudge with your own leg will make the pony move its hind leg on that side into line.

Front legs
As you ride forward into halt try to make sure that the front legs are in line.

Not listening

Some ponies ignore their rider's aids. Riders do not always give strong enough aids for their ponies, which then plod along sleepily with their noses stuck out. Applying the legs more strongly and shortening the reins will improve the pony's gaits.

Working on the bit

When you are riding a horse or pony it should always be "on the bit." This means that its head is held vertically and its mouth is below the level of the rider's hands. In this position the rider has the best possible control over the horse. It can be difficult to achieve and maintain, especially for an inexperienced rider and a pony that may not be perfectly schooled, but you can do it with practice.

Head position
The pony is holding its head just behind the vertical, but it is striding out well.

Walk to halt and halt to walk

This is achieved by pressure from your legs and on the reins and shifting your weight in your seat. Although your lower legs and your hands—via the reins—should always be in contact with the pony, increasing or decreasing that contact tells it what you want it to do. Once the pony has obeyed your aids, relax them.

1 To ask a pony to walk, sit up straight, and "feel" the pony's mouth by gently tightening the reins. Move your weight forward, and squeeze its sides with your lower legs behind the girth.

3 Try to get the pony to halt squarely. Although you have stopped do not completely relax your position. Maintain contact with your legs and hands to keep the pony alert.

2 To halt, sit down deep in the saddle, and lean your weight backward slightly. To stop the pony from moving forward, resist the movement with your hands and the reins.

4 To move off into a walk again, press your legs more firmly into the pony's sides, and relax the reins a little to let it walk forward. Then relax your aids, but maintain contact.

Turning left and right

When you are turning a pony, your outside leg and inside hand—that is your right leg and left hand if you are turning left—produce the movement. They are supported by the inside leg, which keeps the pony steady, and the outside hand, which reinforces the inside hand. The pony should not wander forward while turning.

Your left hand moves back toward the pony's saddle.

View from above

When you look down on a pony and its rider as they turn, you can see how much the pony's body bends around the rider's inside leg. The rider's body shifts as it follows the pony's, and their head turns so that it faces the way they are going.

The left rein is gently pulled back to turn the pony's head.

Your right leg starts the movement with pressure behind the girth.

Your right hand is held close to the pony's neck.

The right rein supports the left rein by pressing against the neck.

The pony's bit is pulled to the left by the left rein.

1 Starting from a halt, press your right leg into the pony's side behind the girth, and gently pull your left rein back.

Turning left

When you are turning left, the pony's front legs and right hind leg move around its left hind leg. As soon as you have completed the turn you should drive the pony forward to a walk or trot in a straight line.

2 Keep your left leg near the girth. Bring the right rein over to press on the pony's neck.

3 As it starts to turn the pony's front legs move in a semicircle around its hind legs.

4 Continue to apply your hand and leg aids until you have turned the pony as far as you want to go.

1 Begin by pressing your left leg against the pony's side just behind the girth.

Turning right

In a turn to the right the pony's front legs and left hind leg move around its right hind leg. Its neck and spine bend in the direction of the movement.

2 Feel the right rein to turn the pony's head by bringing your hand back slightly.

3 Move your left hand toward the right to press the left rein against the pony's neck.

4 Continue to drive the pony around with your left leg. Try not to let it step forward as it turns.

Practicing a posting trot

Before you learn to trot practice posting with the horse standing still. Take your weight on your feet in the stirrups, stand for a moment, and then sit down again. If you feel unsteady, rest your hands on the front of the saddle or on the horse's withers.

Stand up in the stirrups, keeping your knees slightly bent and taking your weight on the balls of your feet.

Lower yourself gently down to sit back in the saddle again. Do not let yourself flop down with a bump.

Learning to trot

The trot is a two-beat gait in which the pony's legs move in diagonal pairs: left fore and right hind, right fore and left hind. Because of this, it is very bumpy for the rider. To even out the bumps you post, or rise to the trot, most of the time. But for more advanced riding you also have to learn to sit to the trot. This is more difficult to do.

Posting trot

To post you take your weight off the saddle by standing in the stirrups as one pair of the pony's legs moves forward. Then sit down again as the opposite pair of legs moves. Try not to rise too high. At first it is difficult to get the rhythm right.

Changing the diagonal

When you post, you are said to be riding on either the right or the left diagonal, according to which pair of the pony's feet touches the ground as you sit in the saddle. To change the diagonal, you simply sit for an extra beat and then continue posting again. You should change the diagonal when you change the rein (see page 49) and alternate when outside of the arena.

On the left diagonal the rider sits in the saddle as the pony's left forefoot and right hind foot hit the ground. Most people ride on the left diagonal when they are trotting a circle to the right.

On the right diagonal the rider sits in the saddle as the pony's right forefoot and left hind foot hit the ground. Most people ride on the right diagonal when they are trotting a circle to the left.

Sitting trot

To sit to the trot, you must keep your seat and your thighs in contact with the saddle all the time and not bump around. You need good balance to do this, and you must relax the lower part of your back and allow it to absorb the pony's movements.

Transitions

A change of gait is called a transition. Going faster is an upward transition, going more slowly is a downward transition. To carry out transitions successfully you need impulsion, which is the energy you create in the pony by using the aids.

From walk . . .
Start with a good walk with the pony striding forward full of energy. To ask for trot, shorten your reins, squeeze with your legs behind the girth, and push with your seat. As the pony moves forward into a trot, ease your aids.

. . . to trot
As the pony starts to trot relax your reins a little to allow it to move forward, but maintain contact. If it seems to want to go back to walk, you will need to reapply your legs to keep it going. If necessary, use a crop.

Trotting
Once the pony gets into its stride you need to keep it trotting with a good, even rhythm. Keep contact with your hands and legs. How strong this contact must be will depend on how forward-going the pony is.

From trot . . .
To carry out a downward transition from trot to walk, sit deep in the saddle and squeeze with your legs behind the girth to drive the pony forward into its bit. At the same time, resist the forward movement with your hands.

. . . back to walk
When the pony slows down to walk, relax your aids, but still maintain contact with your legs and hands. You may still need to drive it forward to get a good, free-striding walk, and you still need to maintain impulsion.

Cantering

T he canter is a wonderful gait once you have learned how to sit to it. At first you will bump out of the saddle, which is uncomfortable. To sit to the canter, you must keep in contact with the saddle, and at the same time try and relax.

Tips for cantering

Before you give the aids to canter the pony has to be going forward well and be balanced. This will be in trot when you are learning. You must drive the pony forward with your legs and control the energy with your hands— do not let it trot faster and faster and become unbalanced.

Try to relax the lower part of your back when you canter so you can follow the pony's movements.

Do not lean forward out of the saddle because the pony may interpret this as a signal to go faster.

Keep your reins fairly short, and maintain contact with the pony's mouth so it cannot get its head down.

The aids

To canter on the right lead, squeeze with your left leg behind the girth and tighten your right rein. Keep your right leg pressed into the pony on the girth. Reverse the aids in order to canter on the left lead.

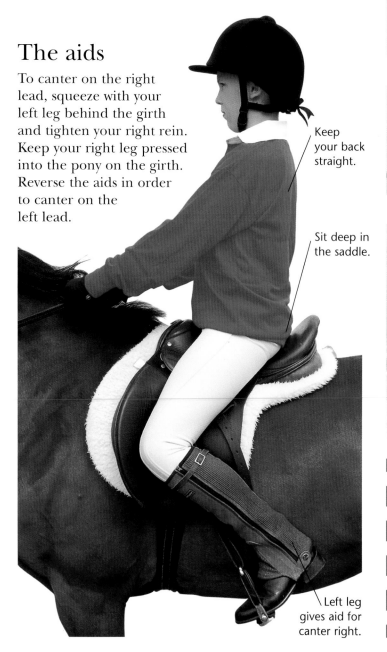

Keep your back straight.

Sit deep in the saddle.

Left leg gives aid for canter right.

The pony should be light on its feet when it is cantering.

The gait

A canter is a three-beat gait in which the horse's front and hind legs on one side are farther forward than those on the other. The horse is said to be leading with, or on, the right or the left leg. When it is on the right leg, its feet hit the ground in the following sequence: left hind, right hind and left front together, right front. After this there is a moment of suspension when all the feet are off the ground at the same time. A well-schooled horse can change lead in the air. This is called a flying change.

Good working canter

The working canter is the gait you will learn when you first start cantering. Traveling at average speed, the pony should move freely with good rhythm and respond to your aids at all times.

Keep a good contact on the reins so that you stay in control.

Keep the pony cantering with pressure from your right leg.

The pony's weight is on its left front leg and right hind leg.

This pony is cantering with its right leg leading.

Checking the lead

You should be able to feel which leg is leading while cantering because the pony's shoulder on that side will be slightly farther forward than its other shoulder. But when you are first learning, you may need to take a quick look down to check.

The ears laid back show that the pony is unhappy.

You are thrown off balance.

Your seat is thrown out of the saddle.

The right hind leg leads.

The left foreleg leads.

ght fore leading
e right hind and left fore just hitting the ground.

Right fore leading
All the pony's weight is now put on the right foreleg.

In the air
For a brief moment all the pony's legs are in the air.

Cross cantering

When a pony leads with one front leg and the opposite hind leg while cantering, it is said to be cross cantering. It is uncomfortable for both the pony and the rider. If it happens, go back to a trot and give the aids to canter again.

Western riding

Seat position
Sit down in the deepest part of the saddle with your ear, shoulder, hip, and heel aligned. Keep your heels down.

How to hold the reins
Separate the reins with your index finger, and hold them above and in front of the saddle's horn.

Leg position
Ride with a nearly straight leg and a fairly long stirrup, letting your legs hang down lightly by the horse's sides.

W hen riding western, you use only the lightest of touches to tell the horse what to do. When it has obeyed your aids and is carrying out your wishes, you sit still and do nothing. You do not need to keep in contact with its mouth, but hold the reins very lightly, except when giving specific aids. You can use your voice as an aid to tell it to change gaits and to halt.

Legs, seat, and hands

You should sit up tall and straight in the saddle, yet be in a relaxed position. Rest the balls of your feet in the stirrups. You hold your hands higher than you would in English-style riding, at approximately the level of your elbows. When you are riding western, you may hold the reins in one hand or two, except in competitions.

Turning left

Giving the aids for turning with the reins in one hand only is called neck-reining. The rein on the inside of the turn makes the horse look in the direction it is going. The rein on the outside puts pressure on its neck, telling it to move over.

1 Move your right hand to the left, so the left rein turns the horse's head in the correct direction and the right rein presses against its neck.

2 Look in the direction in which you want to go. At the same time relax your left leg and push the horse over to the left with your right leg.

Turning right

When you are turning right, the right rein turns the horse's head to the right, and the left rein presses against its neck to tell it to move to the right. Your right leg relaxes, and your left leg pushes the horse over.

1 The right rein starts the movement, and the left rein presses against the horse's neck.

2 Look toward the right, and push the horse over with your left leg until the turn is completed.

Walk, jog, halt

Western riding is based on a system of ask and release. You ask the horse to move forward or stop using your legs, reinforced by your reins and voice (if necessary). As soon as the horse obeys, you relax the aids. This release is its reward. As the horse moves into a faster gait its head will rise. As it does this take up some of the slack in the reins, but do not pull on the horse's mouth.

Walk on
To ask a horse to walk forward using western aids, apply pressure with your lower legs to its sides. If it does not obey at first, make a clucking noise while using your legs.

Jog
This is a kind of slow trot. Ask the horse to jog with your leg aids, reinforced with a clucking noise (if necessary), and shorten the reins slightly as the horse's head rises.

Halt
Push your weight down into your heels, and brace your body while saying, "Whoa." If the horse does not obey, raise your reins a little to put pressure on the bit. Repeat the rein aid if necessary.

In the
arena

When you have learned how to ride at the basic gaits and can control a pony on your own, you will progress to carrying out various exercises in the arena. These will improve your skills and make you a better rider.

A group lesson
In a group lesson you have to keep up with the pace of the pony in front of you and keep your pony's mind on its work.

Passing shoulder to shoulder

While you are riding in the school you may have to ride past another pony and rider. When you do this, you should pass left shoulder to left shoulder. This is also the generally accepted way of passing another rider you may meet when on a trail ride.

Riding at the correct distance

When you are riding in a group you must leave a pony's length between your pony and the pony in front of you. Riding close behind another pony may upset it, and it might kick out at your own pony and injure it or you.

Riding in a group

Riding in a group can be a challenge at first. There are many things to remember. You must control your own pony, but at the same time consider what other riders are doing. Your pony may behave differently, too, in the company of others. It may be more excitable or it may refuse to leave the other ponies to carry out your wishes. You will learn both from your own riding and from watching others.

Exercises in the arena

Carrying out individual exercises in the arena that involve changes of gait and direction, such as riding circles and loops, is a good way of testing your riding ability. You have to manage your pony and give the correct aids at the right time. Your instructor will help you if you need assistance.

Riding exercises in pairs

If you have four or more riders in your group, you can carry out exercises in pairs. This is fun to do, and it is also a great test of timing and judgment. You have to be level with each other all the time, which is difficult if one pony has a longer stride than the other. You might ride up the arena, circle in opposite directions, then pair up again. With practice you can do this at a trot and a canter.

Dressage arena

Most arenas are marked out with letters like a dressage arena. You can use the letters as points at which to change your direction or gait. For example, you might walk from K to H, trot to F, and so on. To remember the sequence of the letters, use a phrase like "All King Edward's Horses Can Make Big Fences."

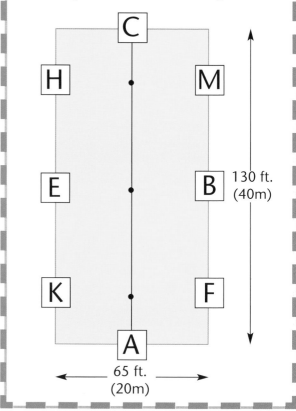

130 ft. (40m)

65 ft. (20m)

Changing gaits

If you are told to walk to H and then trot to M, you should break into a trot as your pony's shoulder becomes level with the letter. It is a challenge, and your pony must be well balanced and obedient to your aids. You have to judge exactly the right moment to give the aids, and you have to deliver them precisely. This takes a lot of practice.

Figures to ride

The top row of figures shows ways of changing the rein—altering the direction in which you are riding around the arena. Some of the other figures also involve a change of rein. The aim is to make all these shapes as accurate as possible. A circle should be round, not flattened. A figure eight should be made up of two equal circles. The loops of a serpentine should also be of equal size.

Ride up the center from the right rein, and then turn left to change the rein.

Ride across the center of the arena, and then turn left to change the rein.

Ride across a short diagonal, such as from M to E or from corner to corner.

Riding a two-loop serpentine across the center is another way of changing the rein.

A 16 ft. (5m) loop is a curve that goes up to 16 ft. (5m) in from the long side of the school.

You can ride circles of 30 and 60 ft. (10 and 20m) in diameter from a number of points.

Riding a figure eight's two complete circles involves two changes of rein.

Riding a three-loop serpentine leaves you going in the same direction as you started.

Riding a four-loop serpentine means you end up going around in the opposite direction.

Whole ride no stirrups

When you have riding lessons, you may spend part of each session riding without stirrups. To stop them from banging against the pony's sides, you cross them over in front of the saddle. The group may walk or trot around together, or you may take turns to trot around while the rest of the group walks.

Without stirrups and reins

Once you have had a few riding lessons you may be asked to ride without stirrups and later without reins. Riding without stirrups is an excellent way of improving your seat in the saddle. Riding without reins improves your balance. You should never rely on the reins to keep your balance.

Lungeing without reins

When riding without reins, you should tie them in a knot in front of the horse's withers to stop them from hanging loose. When you are on a lunge line, you do not have to worry about steering or stopping the horse, although you will learn to change direction using your legs.

Walk on the lunge
You can concentrate on your position in the saddle and use the leg aids to control the horse's pace and direction.

Trot on the lunge
You may feel insecure when trotting. If so, hold on to the front of the saddle or a neck strap with one or both hands.

Without stirrups

Let your legs hang down beside the pony. Keep them pressed against its sides with your heels down and your toes up.

Try to sit deep down in the saddle and not bump out of it.

Relax your back so you can follow the pony's movements.

Riding without stirrups is hard work on your muscles, and your legs will ache afterward.

Holding on to the saddle

When you first ride without stirrups, you will probably hold on to the front of the saddle with one hand while you hold the reins with the other. Your instructor may take you on a lead line or on the lunge until you become more experienced.

The instructor will lead your pony very slowly at first to let you get used to being without stirrups.

Sit up straight as if you had stirrups.

If you hold both reins in one hand, keep it in the correct position.

Without reins

Riding without reins is a test of balance. An experienced rider should be able to ride independently of the reins.

Using your leg aids, practice turning the pony right and left.

If you lose your balance, hold the saddle or neck strap.

If your pony misbehaves or tries to run off, take hold of the reins immediately.

Trot on your own

When you have become more experienced at riding without stirrups, you will be allowed to ride on your own. You can walk, trot, canter, and even jump without stirrups. You will need to use both hands on the reins, but if you feel unsafe, you could rest your hands, still holding the reins, on the front of the saddle. You have to keep contact with the pony's mouth.

Forward and back

Keep your seat in the saddle with your legs in the correct position. Then lean forward to touch the horse's head behind its ears or as far as you can reach. Go back to your starting position, and then lean back to touch the top of the horse's tail, twisting at the waist as you do so. Do not pull on the horse's mouth.

Around the world

In this exercise you go around in a complete circle while sitting on the horse. As you move around steady yourself by holding on to the saddle.

Exercises in the saddle

Doing stretching and twisting exercises on your pony is fun. They will help make you supple, and once you have had a bit of practice doing them you will become a more confident rider. Start all the exercises by sitting in the correct position in the saddle (see pages 30–31). Only practice the exercises when you have someone with you who can hold your pony.

1 Tie your reins in a knot on the horse's neck, and take both your feet out of the stirrups.

2 Lift your right leg over the horse's neck—be careful not to kick it as you do so.

3 Swing your left leg over the quarters. Hold the saddle with your right hand.

4 You are now facing backward. It feels strange without the horse's neck in front!

5 Start going back by twisting around and swinging your right leg over the horse's back.

6 Hold on to the front and the back of the saddle as you sit on the horse facing sideways.

7 Shift yourself around in the saddle as you prepare to move your left leg back over again.

8 Swing your left leg back over the horse's neck to return to where you started.

Arm exercises

Stretch your arms high up in the air, and then rest your hands on your shoulders. Stretch both your arms out to the sides, and bring your hands back to your shoulders. Reach forward, and then go back again.

Leg stretching

Sit in the correct position in the saddle, and keep the upper part of your legs still. Swing your left leg forward as far as you can, moving it from the knee down. Then swing it back as far as you can. Repeat the exercise with your right leg. Now bring both legs back to the usual position. Moving one at a time, point your feet down as far as they will go and then up to stretch your ankles.

Leaning back

You may need to hold on to the front of the saddle to do this exercise but try to manage without doing so. Simply lean right back until your head is resting on the pony's quarters. Stay there for a moment or two, and then sit up again. This is a good way of developing the strong stomach muscles you need for riding.

Touching toes

Lift your right hand up in the air, and then bend down over the left side of your saddle and touch your left toe. Straighten up again and repeat the exercise, lifting your left hand up and bending down to touch your right toe.

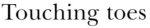

Your first jumping lessons

Approach
The approach to a jump is very important. You must drive the pony firmly forward with pressure from your legs.

Learning to jump is very exciting. There is a lot to learn, but if you ride correctly over trotting poles and small fences, in time big fences will not be a problem. The pony must be moving with impulsion before takeoff, and you have to follow its movement over the jump.

Leading over poles

First jumping lessons for both ponies and riders are usually over poles laid on the ground and spaced out so the pony can walk and trot over them. To begin with, your instructor may lead your pony over them.

Jumping position

For jumping you need to learn the jumping position. When jumping, shorten the stirrups a hole or two. Lift your bottom clear of the saddle and lean forward, putting your weight on your knees and on your feet in the stirrups.

The half-seat position

You use the half-seat position when galloping to take the weight off the horse's back. Shorten your reins, and keep your knees pressed into the saddle and your heels down. If your heels come up, you will lose your balance.

1 As you approach the poles shorten your reins slightly and get into jumping position. Drive the pony on with your legs. Keep your heels down and your head up, and look ahead to where you are going.

2 The pony will lift up its feet to trot over the poles. It should move smoothly and evenly with a regular rhythm and not jump over the poles. Use a posting trot when you are trotting over poles.

Trotting over poles

Trotting over poles is a good exercise for a pony. Lay three or four poles 3–3.5 ft. (1–1.3m) apart, according to the pony's size. When the spacing is correct, the pony's hind foot will hit the ground halfway between two of the poles.

Keep your legs in contact
with the pony's sides and your heels down during the jump. Feel the reins, but do not pull.

Takeoff
When the pony's hind legs propel it into the air, lean forward to go with the pony's movement. Let your hands follow its head.

1 Walk over the poles at first. Go around the arena, and try approaching them from both directions. Use jumping position as you ride over the poles.

2 When you are happy in walk, trot around the arena, and as you go around concentrate on the row of poles. Keep a good rhythm in the trot, and look ahead as you ride—not at the poles.

Your first jump

After trotting poles, you will learn to take your first jump. It will not be very high. Crossed poles encourage the pony to jump in the center, where the fence is lower. Wings placed at each side of a jump help prevent the pony from avoiding it and running out. This counts as a refusal in competitions.

Landing
When the pony lands, keep the forward position and make sure you do not pull on its mouth.

Sequence of a jump

A jump can be divided into four parts: the approach, takeoff, suspension in the air, and landing. You can approach a jump in a trot or a canter—both must be balanced and rhythmical. The takeoff has to be at the right distance for the horse to clear the fence. Once the pony has landed, do not hesitate. Ride it straight on toward the next fence.

Looking forward

Once you have learned to ride you can enjoy many activities. You might join a pony club or go away to a riding camp. You can go on trail rides with friends and take part in horse shows and gymkhanas.

Hand signals on the road

Give clear signals to pedestrians and cyclists as well as drivers, leaving plenty of time before you carry out your intended movement. Hold your reins firmly in the other hand to keep control of your pony.

Turning right
When you wish to turn right, first check behind you that no vehicle is approaching. Hold your right arm out straight to give the signal. Check that it is safe to turn before you do so.

Turning left
To turn left, check for approaching vehicles, and then hold your left arm out straight to give the signal. Before you make the turn check again that it is safe for you to do so.

Thank you
To thank a driver who slows down for you, raise a hand and smile. If you do not wish to take a hand off the reins, nod your head and smile at the driver.

Stop
If you wish to ask another road user to stop, hold up your right hand in front of you. Do not be afraid of asking drivers to stop or slow down if necessary.

Riding safely on the road

Always ride on the correct side of the road, and keep to the inside. Never ride more than two abreast, and stick to single file on narrow lanes. If you are riding two abreast, then the rider on the inside of a turn to the left or right should make the hand signal.

Road safety

Before you ride on the road learn the systems of rules and signals that apply. If possible, take a road safety test. Make sure you can control your pony in all situations. Avoid riding on main roads and narrow roads that do not have grass shoulders. Never ride on the road at night or when it is foggy.

Asking traffic to slow down
To ask a driver to slow down, hold your outside arm out to the side and move it slowly up and down. Thank them when they do slow down.

Light-reflective equipment

You should never ride on a road at night, but on gray, winter afternoons you can wear light-reflecting safety gear. You can buy a reflective belt, hat cover, and vest for yourself as well as a bridle cover, leg bands, tail guard, and exercise sheet for your pony. You can also buy lights that clip to your stirrups, showing a white light at the front and red at the back.

Safety vest

A safety vest is worn over your outdoor clothes. It may have a light-reflective strip across the back and front, or it may feature a warning to other road users such as "Caution: horse and rider" or "Please pass wide and slow."

Reflective strip

Safety vest

Trail riding

Trail riding—riding ouside of the arena—with friends is fun. If you plan your route beforehand, you can make the ride more interesting. You might explore woods and meadows—using fallen logs as jumps—canter along a trail, or even ford a shallow stream. Tell an adult where you are going and when you expect to return.

Riding across open ground

It is fun to canter or gallop across open ground if you are allowed to, but make sure that you can control your pony before you start. Go uphill if possible, and stay at least a pony's length away from other horses.

Opening and closing gates

A gate on a trail should have a latch that you can reach when mounted. You should then be able to open the gate, walk through it, and close it without dismounting. Practice at the stable before you try it on a trail.

1 Ride right up to the gate and position your pony alongside it so you can reach out to work the latch.

2 Lean forward to release the latch. Keep your pony standing still with the reins in your other hand.

3 Push the gate open, and hold on to it while you ride through. Do not let it swing back on your pony.

4 Once through the gate, turn your pony around and close it again. Make sure the gate is securely shut.

Riding on trails

In some areas you may be able to use trails specifically designed for horseback riders. When riding on one of these trails, follow the signposts and do not stray from the track if it crosses a meadow. Watch out for farm animals, and make sure that any gates you may go through are closed and properly secured.

Riding past other animals

You may ride past a pasture in which other horses, or cattle, charge and upset your pony. Try to keep your pony calm. Keep your reins short, and use your legs strongly to ride past them.

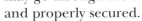
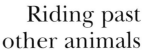

Riding a pony through water

Only cross a stream if you know the water is shallow. Many ponies are nervous of water unless they know that there is firm ground beneath it. Let the pony take its time at first, but then drive it on firmly with your legs and seat.

Ready to move on

As your riding improves you can progress. You might learn dressage or how to improve your jumping until you are good enough to enter competitions. If you enjoy galloping and riding cross–country, you might compete in hunter paces or eventing. Whatever your aim, you will need to work hard to achieve it.

Turn on the forehand

The pony turns through 180 degrees with its hind legs and outside front leg moving around the inside front leg. To perform a turn on the forehand to the right, feel the right rein and keep the contact with the left rein. With your right leg behind the girth, push the pony's hindquarters around step by step. Keep your left leg in contact behind the girth throughout the turn.

Going faster

Only gallop when you are sure you can control your pony. If you are with other ponies and riders, spread out and leave plenty of space between you. Try to gallop uphill because it is then much easier to stop. Go into half-seat position (see page 54), and keep your reins short.

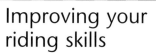

Improving your riding skills

No matter how good a rider you are, there is always more to learn.
Try to ride a variety of ponies—they will teach you a lot.
Never forget the basic principles of riding and handling horses and ponies.

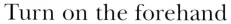

Competitive riding

You may be happy to spend your time pleasure riding, but you might want to compete. Whatever kind of equestrian sport you wish to enter, your pony must be healthy, well schooled, and obedient. Even if jumping is your aim you will have to spend a lot of time doing flat work to prepare it for competitions.

Show jumping
You may aim to become a top-class show jumper, but you will have to start by entering novice competitions at local shows. Your pony must be a careful jumper, and you need to be able to plan your round and remember the course.

Cross-country
To succeed in eventing or hunter paces, you must be a bold and confident rider. You need a fast pony with the stamina to keep on galloping, even though it may be tired, and the courage to tackle fences at high speeds.

Dressage competitions
Dressage is an extension of the work you do in the arena. You need to work hard at perfecting the pony's gaits and transitions, and you have to be able to give accurate and strong aids. You can start competing at pony club level.

It may look easy, but both horse and rider are working very hard!

If your pony does not obey you, ask yourself if you gave the aids clearly enough and try again.
Whatever kind of riding you are doing, be decisive in your actions; do not hesitate.
When you are jumping, apart from going into jumping position, try to keep still in the saddle.
Do not overface your pony or work it so hard it gets stale. Go on a trail ride for a change of scenery.
Keep your hands still and relaxed, except when you are giving specific aids.

Mounted games
Gymkhanas and some horse shows hold all kinds of games and races in which you can compete either as part of a team or as an individual. You need to be good at games yourself and have a fast pony that can turn quickly.

A small, agile pony is ideal in a gymkhana race.

Glossary

Saddle pad

Mounting block

Y̶ou may not understand all the words you come across as you read about horses and ponies and get to know more about their world. This list explains what some of them mean.

action The way a horse or pony moves.

aids The signals that a rider uses to tell a horse what to do. Natural aids are the rider's legs, **seat**, **hands**, and voice. Artificial aids include crops and spurs.

approach The last few **strides** a horse or pony takes before a jump.

arena A riding ring.

balance A horse is balanced when its weight and that of its rider are distributed so that the horse can move easily and efficiently.

body protector A stiff vest that helps protect your back if you fall off of a horse or pony.

bridoon A **snaffle bit** used with a **double bridle**.

browband The part of a bridle that fits around a horse's or pony's forehead and stops the **headpiece** from slipping back.

cantle The back of a saddle.

changing the rein Changing the direction in which you are riding around the **arena** or show ring.

chaps Leather or suede trousers worn over pants to protect a rider's legs.

cheekpiece The part of a bridle that supports the bit.

cheeks a) The flat sides of a horse's face. b) The vertical side parts of a **curb bit**.

cinch The **girth** on a western saddle.

cob A short-legged, small, stocky horse, usually with a **quiet** temperament.

cob-sized Medium-sized— of a bridle or a halter.

collection Moving with shorter, more elevated strides, thus shortening the horse's or pony's **outline**.

contact The link through the **reins** between a horse's mouth and its rider's **hands**.

crossbred Describes a horse or pony with parents of different breeds.

cross cantering Cantering with one leg leading in front and the opposite leg behind.

curb bit A bit with **cheeks** and a curb chain that acts on a horse's head and chin as well as its mouth.

diagonal a) A pair of the horse's legs diagonally opposite each other (left fore, right hind). b) A slanting line across an **arena**.

double bridle A type of bridle with two bits.

dressage The advanced schooling and training of a horse performed in competitions.

eventing A competition including **dressage**, cross-country, and show jumping.

extension Moving with longer, lower **strides**, thus lengthening the horse's or pony's **outline**.

fender A leather flap that covers the stirrup leather on a western saddle.

flat work The work a horse or pony does on the ground, as opposed to over fences.

flying change Changing the **leading leg** at canter when a horse has all four feet off of the ground.

forehand The head, neck, shoulders, **withers**, and front legs of a horse or pony.

forelock The part of a horse's or pony's mane that falls over its forehead.

gait The **pace** at which a horse or pony moves. The natural gaits are walk, trot, canter, and gallop.

girth The broad strap that goes around a horse's belly to hold the saddle in place.

gymkhana Mounted games and races usually performed as part of a show.

trail ride Riding outside

of the **arena**.

hackamore A type of bitless bridle that may be used in western riding.

half chaps **Chaps** that extend from the ankle to just below the knee.

hands a) The units to measure a horse's or pony's height. One hand equals 4 in. (10cm). b) A rider who has light but positive control of the **reins** is said to have good hands.

headpiece The part of a bridle or halter that goes over the horse's head.

hunter paces Cross-country jumping competitions.

hunting cap A velvet-covered helmet with a brim.

impulsion The energy a rider creates in a horse by the use of the legs and **seat**.

jodhpur boots Ankle boots worn with **jodhpurs**.

jodhpurs Riding pants that have pads on the inside of the rider's knees.

jog a) A slow trot. b) A **pace** in western riding.

jumping position Leaning forward with the seat off the saddle and taking the weight on the knees and feet; used when jumping.

keeper A small loop on a strap through which the end is put to keep it flat and neat.

Helmet

Measuring stick

Safety vest

Takeoff

Jodhpur boot

landing The stage of a jump when the horse's feet reach the ground again.

leading file The horse and rider at the front of a group.

leading leg The leg that is in front of the others when a horse is cantering.

leg into hand A riding term meaning that you create energy in the horse or pony with your legs and control it with your hands.

leg up An easy way of mounting in which a helper holds the rider's left leg and helps them spring up into the saddle.

loose rein When on a loose rein, the rider has no contact with the horse's mouth.

lungeing Exercising a horse on a long rein that is attached to a special halter.

martingale A piece of **tack** designed to stop a horse from throwing up his head too high. A standing martingale runs from the **noseband** to the **girth**; a running martingale from the **reins** to the girth.

measuring stick A scale used to measure a horse's height.

native pony A breed such as Exmoor, Welsh, or Highland that was bred on the moors and mountains of Great Britain.

near side The left side of a horse or pony.

neck-reining A way of turning used in western riding in which both reins

are held in one hand.

noseband The part of a bridle that goes around a horse's or pony's nose.

off side The right side of a horse or pony.

on the bit A horse's head held in the position in which the rider has the maximum control of it.

outline The shape a horse's or pony's body makes when it is being ridden.

overface To ask a horse to do work, such as jumping, which is beyond its current stage of training.

pace a) Another word for **gait**. b) A gait in which a horse moves both legs on one side together.

poles (for trotting) Poles laid on the ground for training a horse or rider to jump.

pommel The front part of a saddle.

port A raised, half-moon shape in the mouthpiece of a **curb bit** that allows room for the horse's tongue.

quarters The parts of a horse or pony behind the saddle—its hindquarters and hind legs.

quiet Describes a calm horse that is not easily upset.

rein back Stepping back. The horse's legs move in **diagonal** pairs.

reins The parts of a bridle that run from the bit to the rider's hands.

rhythm The evenness and regularity of the horse's or pony's hoof beats.

running out When a horse or pony refuses to jump a fence and goes around the side of it.

saddle pad A saddle-shaped pad used under a saddle to prevent it from rubbing the horse's or pony's back.

safety harness The adjustable straps that hold a helmet in position.

safety vest A vest worn over riding clothes to warn motorists of the rider's presence or that the horse is nervous.

school To exercise a horse for its education and training.

seat a) A rider's position in the saddle. b) The part of the saddle on which a rider sits.

stall A space for a horse in a stable or barn.

helmet A hard hat used for riding.

sluggish Describes a lazy pony that is reluctant to work.

snaffle bit A bit that is usually jointed in the center and has two rings.

stride The distance traveled by a horse's foot between two successive impacts with the ground.

suspension The moment that all of the horse's feet are off the ground at the same time when cantering.

tack All the pieces of saddlery used on a riding horse or pony.

tack room A room where tack is stored. It has bridle hooks and racks for holding saddles.

takeoff The stage of a jump when a horse launches itself into the air.

thoroughbred A breed of horse registered in the General Stud Book. All racehorses are registered thoroughbreds.

throatlash The part of a bridle that goes under the horse's throat and stops the bridle from slipping forward.

trail A path or track where horses and riders are allowed.

transition The change from one **gait** to another. An upward transition is from a slower to a faster pace; a downward transition is from a faster to a slower pace.

waist The narrowest part of a saddle's **seat**.

wings The sides of a jump.

withers The bony ridge at the base of a horse's neck.

working canter A gait between collected and medium canter.

Index

HORSE AND PONY WEBSITES
www.ponyclub.org
(official U.S. Pony Club website)
www.youngrider.com
(links to other horse and pony websites)
www.newrider.com
(advice and information for new riders)
www.ilph.org
(International League for the Protection of Horses website)

Kingfisher would like to thank: Everybody at **The Talland School of Equitation**, especially the Hutton family and Patricia Curtis. Everybody at **Hartpury College Equestrian Centre**, especially Margaret Linington-Payne. Ros Sheppard, western riding consultant.
Models: Tom Alexander, Anna Bird, Blake Christian, Emily Coles, Patricia Curtis, Wesley Davis, Sam Drinkwater, Amelia Ebanks, Naomi Ebanks, Helen Grundy, Sarah Grundy, Charlie Hutton, Pippa Hutton, Hannah James, Olivia Kuropatwa, Sophie Kuropatwa, Margaret Linington-Payne, Rhiannon Linington-Payne, Ella McEwan, Thomas McEwan, Charlotte Nagle, Gemma Oakley, Camilla Tracey, Sawako Yoshii. Lastly, many thanks to Lesley Ward.